CHILDREN'S

HAND CLAP

"Miss Mary Mack" and
42 Other Hand Clapping Games for

D0128879

HAND CLAP!

"Miss Mary Mack" and 42 Other Hand Clapping Games for Kids

by Sara Bernstein

ADAMS MEDIA CORPORATION
Holbrook, Massachusetts

Published by Adams Media Corporation
260 Center Street, Holbrook, MA 02343

ISBN: 1-55850-426-5

Printed in the United States of America.

J I H G F E D C

Library of Congress Cataloging-in-Publication Data
Bernstein, Sara.
    Hand clap! : Miss Mary Mack" and 42 other hand clapping
games for kids / by Sara Bernstein.
        p.   cm.
    ISBN 1-55850-426-5 (pb)
    1. Hand-clapping games—Juvenile literature.
[1. Hand games. 2. Singing games. 3. Games.]   I. Title.
GR481.B47   1994   94-24752
                                                      CIP
                                                       AC

COVER DESIGN: Barry Littmann
COVER PHOTO: Gerda Levy, Leetone Studios, Inc.
ILLUSTRATIONS: Warren Clark

This book is available at quantity discounts for bulk purchases.
For information, call 1-800-872-5627
(in Massachusetts 617-767-8100).

Visit our home page at http://www.adamsmedia.com

*I dedicate this book to my parents and brother,
my very best friends.*

ACKNOWLEDGMENTS

First, and most importantly, my parents, David and Bianca, encouraged my creativity, taught me to be different, and always loved me. My brother, Daryl, let me wreak havoc in his room, caught me before I ran into parked cars when I was learning to Rollerblade, and introduced me to the fun of writing. My grandparents, Marian, Gerda, and Martin, supported me and were always enthusiastic about everything I did. Grandma Gerda donated the services of her photo studio to help me in the production stages of my book. I'd also like to thank my teacher, Ms. Janger, for teaching me how to write and speak well.

I'd like to applaud (get the joke?) a bunch of people who helped me turn an idea into a real book (with pages and everything!). Mike Snell represented me in the big world of publishing. Bob Adams and Brandon Toropov saw the appeal of a cool book on America's most popular kidsport. Dami Santiago and kids around the USA shared their favorite hand-clapping games with me. Brian Shupe and the Boys and Girls Club provided a fun environment where kids could hand-clap to their hearts' delight. Thank you everybody for realizing that hand-clapping is a little step towards friendliness and peace for my generation.

FEB 1 2 1998

TABLE OF CONTENTS

From One Kid to Many More

There are two different kinds of clapping. The grown-up kind is what you do when the orchestra is done playing a Mozart symphony. It's polite and formal. The kids' kind is *hand-clapping*. It's when two kids sing and clap together. It's fast. It's noisy. It's rhythmic. It's fun!

Hand-clapping is the hottest game to arrive on the playground since hopscotch! Kids all over America are singing and clapping to the beat. You've probably done *Miss Suzy Had a Steamboat* or *Miss Mary Mack*, but there are many other hand-clapping games too. In this book, I compiled 43 great ones, with the words, music, and hand motions.

You'll find that some of the songs in here don't make much sense, but they're authentic. I wrote down what kids sing. "The fish ran away with the spoon" is a crazy thought, but the phrase sounds great in the *Fast Food* hand-clapping game!

You can do hand-clapping anywhere: in the car, at a friend's house, in the hall at school, or on the bus. You don't need any supplies except your hands! Most often, two kids hand-clap, but large groups can play the games too.

If you come up with some new hand-clapping games, write them in the blank pages in the *Create Your Own* section of this book. Then copy them on a copy machine, and send them to me. My address is in the back of the book.

Have fun! Happy clapping!

Sara

How to Use This Book

Each hand-clapping game has three main parts: the hand pictures, the music notes, and the words. The games aren't too hard to figure out, but here are some quick instructions in case you need them.

Hand Pictures

The pictures show the hand motions you and your partner do. You read the words from left to right, and for each word you perform the motion at the top of the column.

You'll find that the hand pictures in the hand-clapping games are numbered. That's so you can look them up in the *Basic Hand-Claps* chapter, which describes every hand motion in detail.

If you do hand-clapping in a group, have all the participants stand in a circle. You perform the same motions, only you clap your left hand with the person on your left and your right hand with the person on your right.

Music Notes

Reading the music notes is simple. The higher a note is on the bar, the higher your voice should be when you say the word. The lower a note is on the bar, the lower your voice should be when you say the word.

That's it! No sharps, rests, or anything fancy like that. Don't worry about singing the songs in just the right tone of voice. Try to follow the notes, and sing the songs in a way you think sounds best.

Lyrics

You read the songs from left to right, like a regular story. The words are in columns under the hand pictures and music notes. Many of the words are split up into syllables. You say the word or syllable in the tone of voice of the note above it while doing the hand motion in the picture at the top of the column.

Rhythm and Pacing

This book offers suggestions for hand-clapping. Feel free to work out your own rhythm and pacing for the games. Perform the hand-clapping games however you think sounds best!

BASIC HAND-CLAPS

Each number explains one type of hand-clap. If two movements are described, do both movements at the same time. For instance, in #1, you clap your left hand to your friend's right hand and your right hand to your friend's left hand *at the same time*.

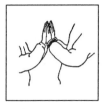

1. You clap your left hand with your friend's right hand and your right hand with your friend's left hand, as if you were pushing a big crate.

2. You clap the back of your left hand with the back of your friend's right hand and the back of your right hand with the back of your friend's left hand, as if you were pushing a big crate with the backs of your hands.

 3. You hold your hands out flat as if you were holding a platter. Your friend claps her left hand with your right hand and her right hand with your left hand.

 4. Your friend holds her hands out flat as if she were holding a platter. You clap your left hand with her right hand and her right hand with your left hand.

 5. You and your friend each clap once, as if you were applauding after a concert.

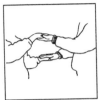

6. You and your friend each hold your left hand out as if you had a handful of sunflower seeds. With your right hand, you each clap the other person's left hand.

7. Like a high-five, you clap your right hand with your friend's right hand at face-level.

8. A left-handed high-five, you clap your left hand with your friend's left hand at face-level.

9. Like a high-five, you clap your right hand with your friend's left hand at face-level.

10. Like a high-five, you clap your left hand with your friend's right hand at face-level.

11. You hold your right hand out flat as if you were holding a book. Your friend claps your right hand with her right hand.

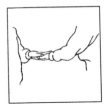

12. You hold your left hand out flat as if you were holding a book. Your friend claps your left hand with her left hand.

13. Your friend holds her right hand out flat as if she were holding a book. You clap her right hand with your right hand.

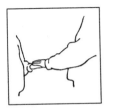

14. Your friend holds her left hand out flat as if she were holding a book. You clap her left hand with your left hand.

15. You clap your right hand with your friend's right hand, as if you both were about to shake hands.

16. You clap your left hand with your friend's left hand, as if you both were about to shake hands.

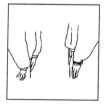

17. You and your friend each clap the front of your own legs, right hand with right leg and left hand with left leg.

18. You and your friend each clap the sides of your own legs where your pockets are, right hand with right leg and left hand with left leg.

19. You and your friend each clap your own knees, right hand with right knee and left hand with left knee.

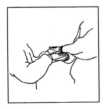

20. You cross your arms and hold your left hand face-down and right hand face-up. Your friend claps her right hand with your right hand and her left hand with your left hand.

21. Your friend crosses her arms and holds her left hand face-up and right hand face-down. You clap your right hand with her right hand and your left hand with her left hand.

22. You clap the back of your right hand with the back of your friend's right hand at shoulder-level.

23. You clap the back of your left hand with the back of your friend's left hand at shoulder-level.

24. You clap your right hand with your friend's left hand at waist-level.

25. You clap your left hand with your friend's right hand at waist-level.

26. You clap your right hand with your friend's right hand at waist-level.

27. You clap your left hand with your friend's left hand at waist-level.

28. You clap your right hand with your friend's left hand and your left hand with your friend's right hand up in the air over your heads.

29. You and your friend each stretch out your arms as if you were describing a really big hippopotamus. You clap your right hand with your friend's left hand and your left hand with your friend's right hand.

30. You clap your right hand with your friend's left hand and your left hand with your friend's right hand at slightly below waist-level, as if you were pushing a big crate.

31. You and your friend turn around so you are back-to-back. You clap your right hand with your friend's left hand and your left hand with your friend's right hand at slightly below waist level.

32. Just like a high-five, you clap your right hand with your friend's right hand in the air above your heads.

33. Just like a high-five, only lefty, you clap your left hand with your friend's left hand in the air above your heads.

34. You hold your right hand up like you're taking an oath. Your friend claps her right hand with your right hand.

35. You hold your left hand up like you're taking an oath. Your friend claps her left hand with your left hand.

36. Your friend holds her right hand up like she's taking an oath. You clap your right hand with her right hand.

37. Your friend holds her left hand up like she's taking an oath. You clap your left hand with her left hand.

38. You and your friend both cross your arms. You make your palms face in, and your friend makes her palms face out. You clap your right hand to your friend's left hand and your left hand to your friend's right hand.

39. You clap your right hand with your friend's right hand and your left hand with your friend's left hand, with the right hands above.

40. You clap your left hand with your friend's left hand and your right hand with your friend's right hand, with the left hands above.

41. You clap your right hand with your friend's right hand and the back of your left hand with the back of your friend's left hand, with the right hands above.

42. You clap the back of your left hand with the back of your friend's left hand and your right hand with your friend's right hand, with the left hands above.

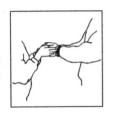

43. You hold your hands together, as if you were applauding after a concert. Your friend claps her hands with your hands in between.

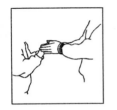

44. Your friend holds her hands together, as if she were applauding after a concert. You clap your hands with your friend's hands in between.

45. You hold up your right elbow, as if you were showing off your muscle. Your friend claps her right hand with the inside of your right elbow.

46. You hold up your left elbow, as if you were showing off your muscle. Your friend claps her left hand with the inside of your left elbow.

47. Your friend holds up her right elbow, as if she were showing off her muscle. You clap your right hand with the inside of your friend's right elbow.

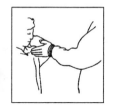

48. Your friend holds up her left elbow, as if she were showing off her muscle. You clap your left hand with the inside of your friend's left elbow.

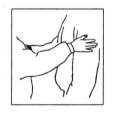

49. You clap your right hand with your friend's left shoulder, and your friend claps her right hand with your left shoulder.

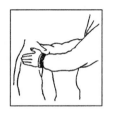

50. You clap your left hand with your friend's right shoulder, and your friend claps her left hand with your right shoulder.

51. You and your friend both raise your right knees, as if you were marching. You both clap your right hands with your right knees.

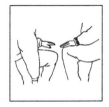

52. You and your friend both raise your left knees, as if you were marching. You both clap your left hands with your left knees.

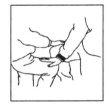

53. You and your friend both raise your right knees, as if you were marching. You clap your right hand with your friend's right knee, and your friend claps her right hand with your right knee.

 54. You and your friend both raise your left knees, as if you were marching. You clap your left hand with your friend's left knee, and your friend claps her left hand with your left knee.

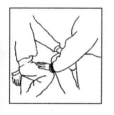 55. You and your friend both raise your right knees, as if you were marching. You clap your left hand with your friend's right knee, and your friend claps her left hand with your right knee.

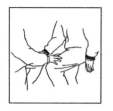 56. You and your friend both raise your left knees, as if you were marching. You clap your right hand with your friend's left knee, and your friend claps her right hand with your left knee.

57. You and your friend each raise your right knee as if you were marching and clap your hands under your right leg.

58. You and your friend each raise your left knee as if you were marching and clap your hands under your left leg.

59. You and your friend each raise your right elbows, as if you were showing off your muscles. You clap the inside of your right elbow with the inside of your friend's right elbow.

60. You and your friend each raise your left elbows, as if you were showing off your muscles. You clap the inside of your left elbow with the inside of your friend's left elbow.

61. You clap your right wrist with your friend's right wrist in the air at face-level.

62. You clap your left wrist with your friend's left wrist in the air at face-level.

63. You and your friend make fists with your right hands. You bop your friend's right fist with your right fist, with your fist on top.

64. You and your friend make fists with your right hands. Your friend bops your right fist with her right fist, with her fist on top.

65. You and your friend make fists with your left hands. You bop your friend's left fist with your left fist, with your fist on top.

66. You and your friend make fists with your left hands. Your friend bops your left fist with her left fist, with her fist on top.

67. You bump your right hip with your friend's left hip.

68. You bump your left hip with your friend's right hip.

69. You poke your friend in the belly-button with your right index finger, and your friend pokes you in the belly-button with her right index finger.

70. You and your friend lightly tap your chests with your right hands, as if you were saying the Pledge of Allegiance.

71. You and your friend lightly tap your chests with your left hands, as if you were saying the Pledge of Allegiance on the wrong side.

72. You and your friend lightly tap your foreheads with your right hands, as if you had a headache.

73. You and your friend lightly tap your foreheads with your left hands, as if you had a headache.

74. You and your friend quickly shake hands with your right hands.

37

75. You and your friend cross your arms over your chests.

76. You and your friend tap the tops of your heads with both hands.

77. You and your friend make thumbs-up signs with both hands and point both thumbs at your chests.

78. On your right hands, you and your friend curl in your middle three fingers and extend your pinkie and your thumb. You both put your right hands next to your faces as if you were talking on the phone.

79. You and your friend snap using the thumb and middle finger on your right hands.

Now turn the page for the
HAND-CLAPPING GAMES!

ANIMAL REPORT

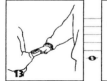			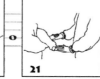	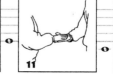	
13	**14**	**5**	**21**	**11**	**12**
We	had	to	read	par-	a-
I	wrote	mine	on	the	gir-
But	when	I	stood	up	to
I	found	I	had	read-	er's
In-	stead	this	is	what	I
Cows	go	moo.			
Mice	make	do.			
Bears	have	fur.			
Cats	say	purr.			

graphs.
affe.
talk,
block.
said:

SARA'S INSIDE TIPS

On the word "moo," make a giant cow sound!

41

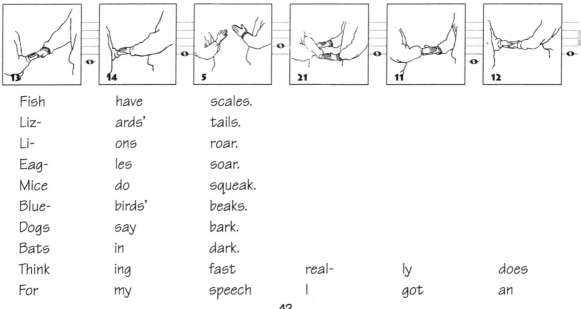

Fish	have	scales.			
Liz-	ards'	tails.			
Li-	ons	roar.			
Eag-	les	soar.			
Mice	do	squeak.			
Blue-	birds'	beaks.			
Dogs	say	bark.			
Bats	in	dark.			
Think	ing	fast	real-	ly	does
For	my	speech	I	got	an

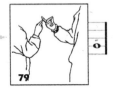

SARA'S INSIDE TIPS

Don't forget to snap your fingers at the end of each line!

pay
A.

BAD LUCK TUCK

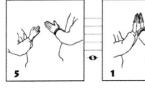   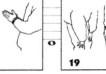

Bad	luck	Tuck	went	for	a
Turned	the	corn-	er,	hit	a
Kept	walk-	ing,	fell	in	a
To	the	park,	tripped	on	a
To	the	shore,	fell	off	a
In	the	sea,	bit	by	a
Set	the	tab-	le,	broke	a
Had	his	string	break	on	his
Tuck,	there's	noth-	ing	go-	ing

44

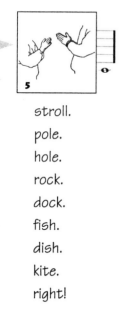

stroll.

pole.

hole.

rock.

dock.

fish.

dish.

kite.

right!

SARA'S INSIDE TIPS

For an extra challenge on any hand-clapping game, try to do it twice as fast!

BATHROOM

The	bath-	room	is
The	per-	fect	place.
I	wash	my	face
And	brush	my	teeth,
Sham-	poo	my	hair,
In	mir-	ror	stare,

46

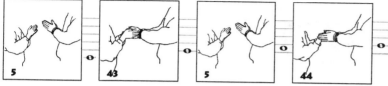

Use	the	toi-	let,
And	clean	my	nails.
If	all	else	fails,
I	soap	my	hands,
Wash	off	the	sand.

BONNIE WIDE

MORE VERSES

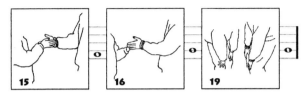

Bon-	nie	Wide
Went	for	a
Ride	ride	ride.
To	fetch	some
Bread	bread	bread.
She	took	wrong
Turns	turns	turns,
Couldn't	find	the
Store	store	store,

48

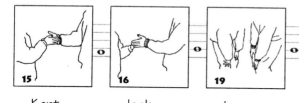

Kept	look-	ing
More	more	more.
She	re-	turned
Home	home	home.
The	bread	was
Stale	stale	stale,
'Cause	the	trip
Took	one	year!

CLEVER MICE

MORE VERSES

 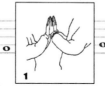   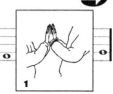

Three	blind	mice!	Three	blind	mice!
See	them	run!	See	them	run!
Chased	by	the	farm-	er's	wife
With	a	big	carv-	ing	knife,
They	ran	un-	der	the	bed.
Farm-	er's	wife	bumped	her	head.

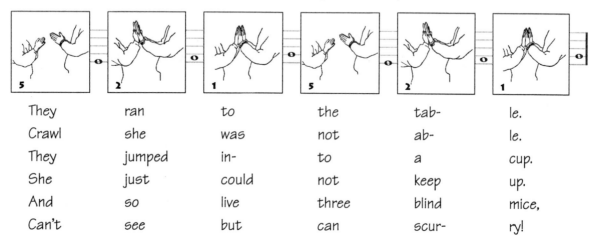

They	ran	to	the	tab-	le.
Crawl	she	was	not	ab-	le.
They	jumped	in-	to	a	cup.
She	just	could	not	keep	up.
And	so	live	three	blind	mice,
Can't	see	but	can	scur-	ry!

COME OUT AND PLAY

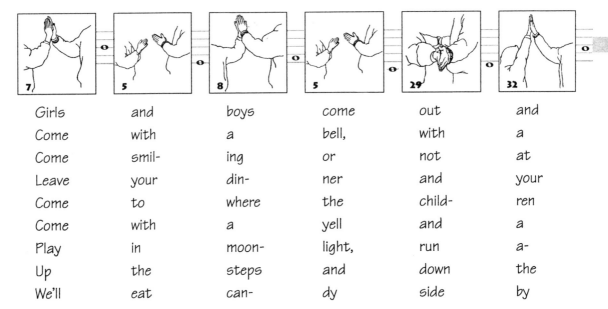

Girls	and	boys	come	out	and
Come	with	a	bell,	with	a
Come	smil-	ing	or	not	at
Leave	your	din-	ner	and	your
Come	to	where	the	child-	ren
Come	with	a	yell	and	a
Play	in	moon-	light,	run	a-
Up	the	steps	and	down	the
We'll	eat	can-	dy	side	by

52

play.
ball.
all.
work,
lurk.
bound.
round.
slide,
side!

SARA'S INSIDE TIPS

On the word "bound," jump in the air! After the phrase "run around," switch places with your partner.

COUNTING TO TEN

One	one	this	is	fun.
Two	two	peek-	a-	boo.
Three	three	tap	your	knee.
Four	four	here	comes	more.
Five	five	yikes!	bee-	hive.

COUNTING TO TEN (CONTINUED)

   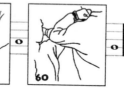

Six	six	cook-	ie	mix.
Seven	seven	up	to	heaven.
Eight	eight	stay	up	late.
Nine	nine	draw	a	line.
Ten	ten	do	it	again!

DILLY DILLY

Lav-	en-	der	blue
Dil-	ly	dil-	ly
Lav-	en-	der	green
When	I	am	king
Dil-	ly	dil-	ly
You	will	be	queen.
Call	up	your	men
Dil-	ly	dil-	ly
Set	them	to	work.

DILLY DILLY (CONTINUED)

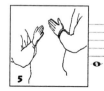   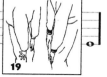

Some	to	the	plow
Dil-	ly	dil-	ly
Some	to	the	cart.
Some	to	make	hay
Dil-	ly	dil-	ly
Some	to	thresh	corn.
While	you	and	I
Dil-	ly	dil-	ly
Keep	our-	selves	warm.

DOWN BY THE BANKS

    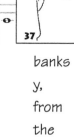 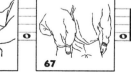

34	35	36	37	39	67
Down	by	the	banks	of	the
Hank-	y	Pank-	y,	where	the
Bull	frogs	jump	from	bank	to
Bank-	y,	where	the	eeps	ops
Tid-	dly	tops,	watch-	in'	the
Bull-	frogs	go	ker-	plop.	

SARA'S INSIDE TIPS

Hand-clapping songs are great for jump-roping too!

Everybody

  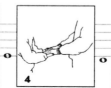 

Tast-	ing	tongue,	breath-	ing	lung
Feet	walk-	ing,	mouth	talk-	ing
Nose	to	pick,	hic-	cups	hick
Bend	el-	bow,	long	hair	grows
Eyes	peer-	ing,	ears	hear-	ing
Fin-	gers	touch,	big	hands	clutch

60

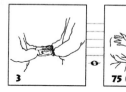   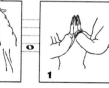 

Heart	beats	thump,	sit	your	rump
Backs	bend-	ing,	bones	mend-	ing
Strong	mus-	cle,	legs	hus-	tle
Think-	ing	brain,	flow-	ing	vein.
All	this	stuff	has	to	keep
work-	ing	even	while	I	sleep.

Everyone's Grumpy

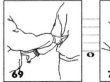 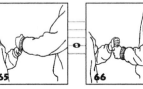

Ev-	e-	ry-	one's
Grum-	py	to-	day.
I	want	to	go
And	get	a-	way.
A	land	where	all
They	do	is	play.
Where	ev-	e-	ry-
One's	hap-	py	and
Has	their	own	way.

FAST FOOD

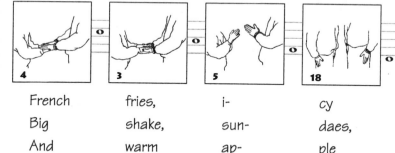

French	fries,	i-	cy	Coke,
Big	shake,	sun-	daes,	fish,
And	warm	ap-	ple	pies.
You	de-	serve	fast	food
To-	day	at	Mc-	Arnolds.
The	fish	ran	a-	way
with	the	spoon	uh	huh
Ya	right	get	down	and
Boog-	ie.			

50 STATES

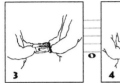    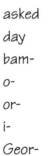

The	test	asked	for	the	50th
But	that	day	I	couldn't	think
Al-	a-	bam-	a,	Al-	as-
Ar-	iz-	o-	na,	Ark-	an-
Cal-	if-	or-	nia,	Colo-	rad-
Conn-	ect-	i-	cut,	Del-	a-
Flor-	ida,	Geor-	gia,	Haw-	a-
Id-	a-	ho,	and	Il-	li-

state.
straight:
ka,
sas,
o,
ware,
ii,
nois.

SARA'S INSIDE TIPS

This song makes it easy to memorize all 50 states in alphabetical order. You can impress your friends and teachers!

50 STATES (CONTINUED)

 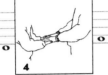 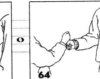 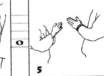 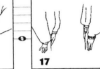

3	4	63	64	5	17
Here	comes	more:	Ind-	i-	a-
Io-	wa,	Kan-	sas,	Ken-	tuck-
Lou-	is-	i-	a-	na,	and
Mar-	y-	land,	Mass-	ach-	u-
Mich-	i-	gan,	Minn-	es-	ot-
Miss-	iss-	ipp-	i,	Miss-	our-
Mont-	an-	a,	Neb-	ras-	ka,
Nev-	a-	da.	New	Hamp-	shire

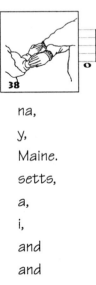

na,

y,

Maine.

setts,

a,

i,

and

and

When you reach your own state's name, yell it out!

SARA'S INSIDE TIPS

50 STATES (CONTINUED)

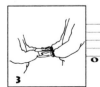 **o** **o** **o** 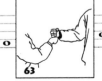 **o**  **o**

3	4	63	64	5	17
New	Jer-	sey,	New	Mex-	i-
New	York,	North	Car-	o-	li-
North	Dak-	o-	ta,	O-	hi-
Ok-	lah-	o-	ma,	Or-	eg-
Penn-	syl-	van-	i-	a,	Rhode
South	Car-	o-	lina,	South	Dak-
Tenn-	ess-	ee,	Tex-	as,	Ut-
Ver-	mont,	Vir-	gin-	ia,	and

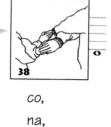

co,

na,

o,

on,

Island,

ota,

ah,

more.

SARA'S INSIDE TIPS

Once you've gotten really good at this game, try it in rounds!

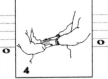 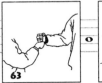  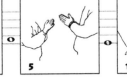 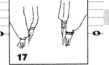

Wash-	ing-	ton,	West	Vir-	gin-
Wis-	con-	sin,	and	I	for-
I	thought	of	for-	ty	nine
the	last	one	I	can't	quite
That's	it!	It's	called	Wy-	o-

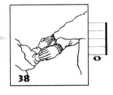

ia,

got.

and

sing.

ming.

SARA'S INSIDE TIPS

See if your Social Studies teacher will give you extra credit for performing 50 States in front of the class.

GOING, GOING, GONE

 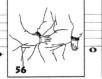

Step	up	to	the	plate	plate
Don't	swing	the	bat	late	late
Hear	all	the	fans	cheer	cheer
No	rea-	son	to	fear	fear.
Here	comes	the	soft-	ball	ball
Wait	for	the	ump's	call	call
He	says	it's	a	strike	strike

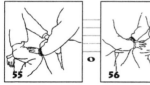 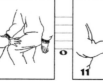   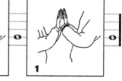

Your	next	thought	is	yikes	yikes.
Here's	the	sec-	ond	one	one
Hit	it	hard	and	run	run
It's	go-	ing	and	gone	gone
To	the	out-	field	lawn	lawn.
It's	a	big	home	run	run
Now	this	game	is	fun	fun.

Ring	ring	ring	ring	ring.
Hel-	lo?	Who	is	it?
Pam-	e-	la	Mc	Cree
Hel-	lo?	Who	is	it?
Vik-	ram	Go-	burd-	hun
Hel-	lo?	Who	is	it?
Car-	los	Gust-	av-	o

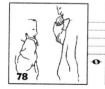

Hel-	lo?	Who	is	it?
Jon-	a-	than	Green-	berg
Hel-	lo?	Who	is	it?
Val-	er-	ie	Ho-	nos
Hel-	lo?	Who	is	it?
E-	liz-	a-	beth	Chen
Let's	talk.	You're	my	friend.

It's Raining

   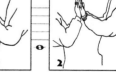

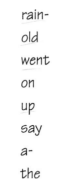 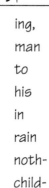

It's	rain-	ing,	it's	pour-	ing.
The	old	man	is	snor-	ing.
He	went	to	bed	with	a
Bump	on	his	head,	could	not
Get	up	in	the	morn-	ing.
We	say	rain	go	a-	way.
Come	a-	noth-	er	day	'cause
All	the	child-	ren	wanna	play.

JIMMY BLIMMY

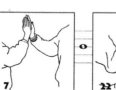 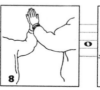 

Jim-	my	Blim-	my
Foot-	ball	foot-	ball
Jim-	my	Blim-	my
Foot-	ball	foot-	ball
Oooh	sha	wa	wa
Found	a	lov-	er
Ice	cream	so-	da
Cher-	ry	on	top

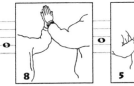 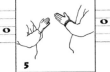

7	22	8	5
Sing-	ing	down	down
ba-	by	down	down
rol-	ler	coast-	er
Sweet	sweet	ba-	by
I	love	you	so
Shim-	my	shim-	my

JIMMY BLIMMY (CONTINUED)

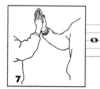   

Co-	co	pop	pop
Shim-	my	shim-	my
Co-	co	pop	pop
Shim-	my	shim-	my
He	missed,	he	missed
He	missed	like	this.

KANGAROO

MORE VERSES ▸

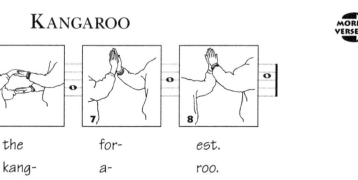

Lives	in	the	for-	est.
Jump	jump	kang-	a-	roo.
Ba-	by	in	pock-	et.
Jump	jump	kang-	a-	roo.
Fuz-	zy	brown	short	fur.
Jump	jump	kang-	a-	roo.

 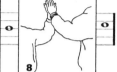

51	52	6	7	8
Strong	legs	for	hop-	ping.
Jump	jump	kang-	a-	roo.
In	Aust-	ral-	i-	a.
Jump	jump	kang-	a-	roo.
Here	comes	a	wild	dog.
Run	run	kang-	a-	roo.

A Loaf of Bread

 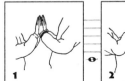 

1	2	5	64	66	3
I	went	to	a	new	bak-
To	buy	a	loaf	of	fresh
They	asked	me	what	my	name
And	so	this	is	what	I
My	name	is	Eli	Eli	Pickle
Pom-	pom	beauty	I'm	a	cut-
Come	and	play	at	three	thir-
We'll	run	and	get	real	dirt-
Sca-	pelli	Thomp-	son	the	fifty-

ery

bread.

was

said:

Pickle

ie.

ty

y.

fourth

SARA'S INSIDE TIPS

The harder you clap hands, the more noise you make!

A LOAF OF BREAD (CONTINUED)

 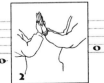   

1	2	5	64	66	3
They	asked	what	bread	I	want-
And	so	this	is	what	I
I	want	the	whole	wheat	sesa-
As-	par-	a-	gus	ba-	nan-
Can-	dy	cane	choc-	o-	late
I	asked	them	what	the	price
And	so	this	is	what	they
The	price	is	twenty-	two	bil-
Six-	ty	five	mil-	lion	and

84

ed
said:
me
a
kind.
was
said:
lion
three!

> **SARA'S INSIDE TIPS**
>
> It's fun to get a family member to videotape your hand-clapping games. Then you can see yourself on TV!

MARIA LUNGRI

 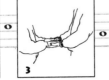 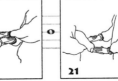 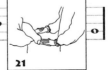

Mar-	i-	a	Lung-	ri.
sat	down	to	din-	ner.
First	French	fries.		
Cher-	ry	pies.		
But-	ter	toast.		
Chick-	en	roast.		
Then	turk-	ey.		
Beef	jerk-	ey.		
An	egg	roll.		

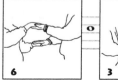 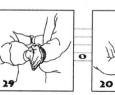 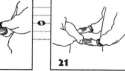

A	rice	bowl.		
Po-	ta-	to.		
To-	ma-	to.		
Tam-	a-	le.		
Soup	split	pea.		
Long	brat-	wurst.		
Juice	for	thirst.		
Mar-	i-	a	Lun-	gri
Was	still	hun-	gry.	

MISS MARY MACK

  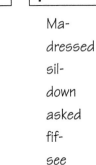 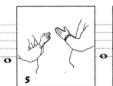  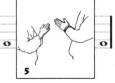

6	1	5	75	17	5
Miss	Ma-	ry	Mack	Mack	Mack
All	dressed	in	black	black	black
With	sil-	ver	buttons	buttons	buttons
All	down	her	back	back	back.
She	asked	her	mother	mother	mother
For	fif-	ty	cents	cents	cents
To	see	the	elephants	elephants	elephants

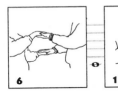   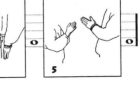

Jump	over	the	fence	fence	fence.
They	jumped	so	high	high	high
They	touched	the	sky	sky	sky.
They	never	came	back	back	back
'Til	the	4th of	July	ly	ly.
You	lie!				

MISS SUZY HAD A BABY

MORE VERSES

Miss	Su-	zy	had	a	baby
His	name	was	Ti-	ny	Tim
She	put	him	in	the	bathtub
To	see	if	he	could	swim
He	drank	up	all	the	water
He	ate	up	all	the	soap

MISS SUZY HAD A BABY

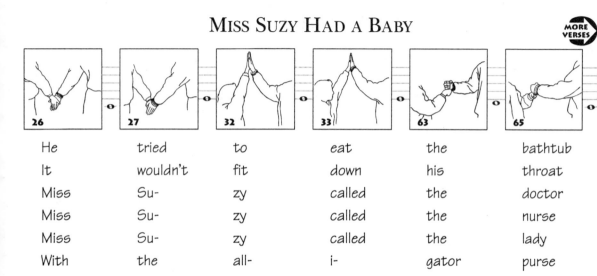

26	27	32	33	63	65
He	tried	to	eat	the	bathtub
It	wouldn't	fit	down	his	throat
Miss	Su-	zy	called	the	doctor
Miss	Su-	zy	called	the	nurse
Miss	Su-	zy	called	the	lady
With	the	all-	i-	gator	purse

MISS SUZY HAD A BABY

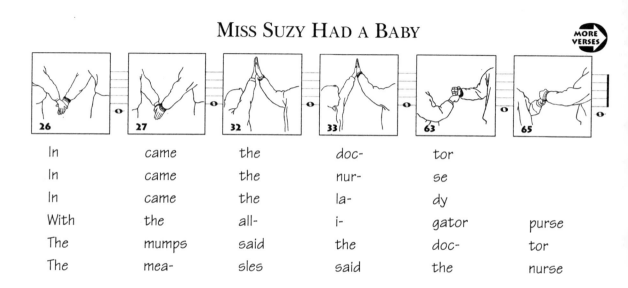

In	came	the	doc-	tor	
In	came	the	nur-	se	
In	came	the	la-	dy	
With	the	all-	i-	gator	purse
The	mumps	said	the	doc-	tor
The	mea-	sles	said	the	nurse

MISS SUZY HAD A BABY

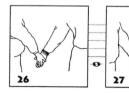 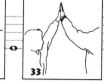 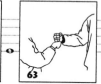 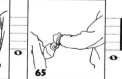

26	27	32	33	63	65
Noth-	ing	said	the	la-	dy
With	the	all-	i-	gator	purse
Good-	bye	to	the	doc-	tor
Good-	bye	to	the	kind	nurse
A	dollar	to	the	la-	dy
With	the	all-	i-	gator	purse

MISS SUZY HAD A STEAMBOAT

     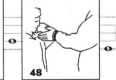

Miss	Su-	zy	had	a	steam-
The	steam-	boat	had	a	bell
Miss	Su-	zy	went	to	Geor-
The	steam-	boat	went	to	Or-
Hell-	o	Ms.	op-	er-	a-
Please	give	me	the	num-	ber
But	if	you	dis-	con-	nect
My	mood	will	not	be	too

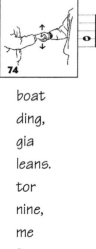

74

boat
ding,
gia
leans.
tor
nine,
me
fine.

SARA'S INSIDE TIPS

After the word "ding," make a tugging motion with your hand as if you were ringing a big bell on a boat!

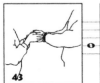   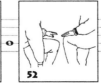 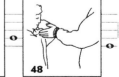

43	44	51	52	46	48
The	dark	is	like	a	mov-
The	mov-	ie	is	like	a
The	show	is	like	a	TV
And	that	is	all	I	know
I	know	I	know	my	ma-
I	know	I	know	my	pa-
I	know	I	know	my	dogg-
With	his	su-	per	claws	claws

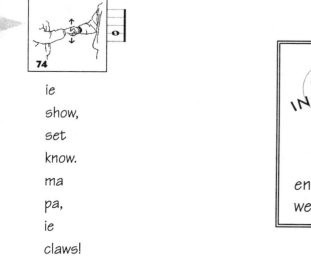

ie
show,
set
know.
ma
pa,
ie
claws!

SARA'S INSIDE TIPS

Miss Suzy Had a Steamboat is one of the most popular hand-clapping games of all time. See if your parents remember it from when they were kids!

MONEY TREE

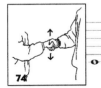

My	best	friend	had
A	mon-	ey	tree.
It	gave	him	coins
And	bills	for	free.
When-	ev-	er	he
Had	wrink-	led	cash,

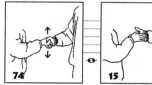 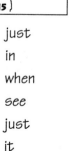 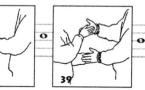

He	just	threw	it
Out	in	the	trash.
But	when	I	came
To	see	mon-	ey,
He	just	laughed	and
Thought	it	fun-	ny.

MOO MOO SPOTTED COW

 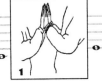   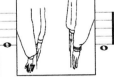

Moo	moo	spot-	ted	cow
Do	you	have	a	mane?
No	sir,	no	sir,	no,
On-	ly	stom-	ach	pains.
Neigh	neigh	fan-	cy	horse
Do	you	have	a	snout?

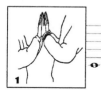 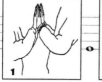  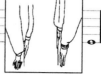

No	sir,	no	sir,	no,
No	with-	out	a	doubt.
Oink	oink	dirt-	y	pig
Do	you	have	some	scales?
No	sir,	no	sir,	no,
I	only	have	a	tail.

NOISES

Cars	zoom.	Bombs	boom.
Hands	clap.	Wings	flap.
Bells	ding.	Phones	ring.
Drums	bong.	Gongs	gong.
Mice	squeak.	Floors	creak.
Games	beep.	Birds	peep.
Bullets	zing.	Balls	ping.
Balloons	pop.	Hammers	bop.
Pots	bang.	Ouch	dang.

SARA'S INSIDE TIPS

You can have a hand-clapping competition with your friends! See which team of two can perform a certain game the best!

P.E. Class

MORE VERSES ▶

   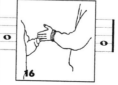

In	P.	E.	class:
Out	to	the	grass
To	ex-	er-	cise
Push	up	and	rise
Ten	jump-	ing	jacks
Stretch	out	our	backs

104

P.E. CLASS (CONTINUED)

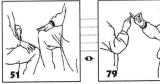 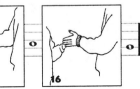

Then	run	a	mile
It	takes	a	while
On	to	a	game
Al-	ways	the	same
Split	in-	to	teams
We	play	and	scream!

RAILROAD CROSSING

MORE VERSES

  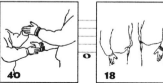

Rail	road	cross	ing
Watch	for	the	cars.
Can	you	spell	it
with-	out	the	Rs?
a	i	l	o
a	d	c	o

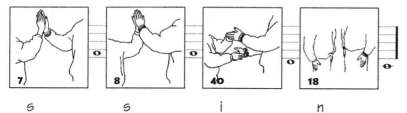

s	s	i	n
g	w	a	t
c	h	f	o
t	h	e	c
a	s		

Rum Tali Rum

Rum	tal-	i	rum	ti	ter-
Tal-	i	rum	ter-	ra	ter-
Ti	ti	ti	a	ti	ti
Ter-	ra	ter-	ra	ti	ter-
Rum	tal-	i	rum	ti	ter-
Tal-	i	rum	ter-	ra	ter-
Ti	ti	ti	a	ti	ter-
Ter-	ra	ter-	ra	ti	ti
A	one	two	three.		

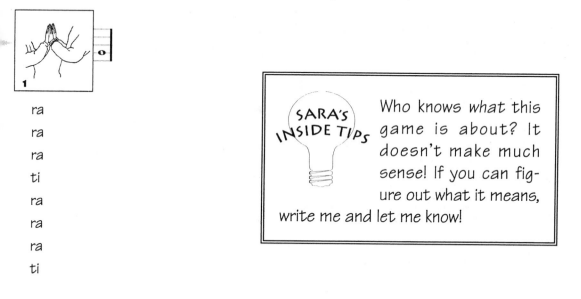

ra

ra

ra

ti

ra

ra

ra

ti

SARA'S INSIDE TIPS Who knows what this game is about? It doesn't make much sense! If you can figure out what it means, write me and let me know!

A SAILOR WENT TO SEA

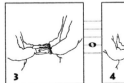 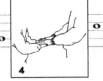  

A	sail-	or	went	to	sea
To	see	what	he	could	see
But	all	that	he	could	see
Was	the	bot-	tom	of	the
Sea	sea	sea.			

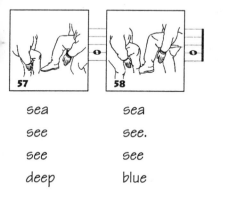

sea   sea

see   see.

see   see

deep   blue

SARA'S INSIDE TIPS

This tune is a tongue-twister! If you hand-clap too fast, you might trip over your words!

SAY, SAY, O, PLAYMATE

  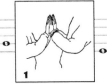 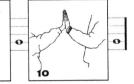

Say,	say	O,	play-	mate
Come	out,	play	with	me.
Bring	your	dol-	lies	three
Climb	my	ap-	ple	tree,
Slide	down	my	rain-	bow
In-	to	my	cel-	lar.
We'll	be	jol-	ly	friends
For-	ever	more	one	two
Three	four	four	four	four.

SARA'S INSIDE TIPS

It's fun to hand-clap in groups. Arrange your friends in a circle. You clap your left hand with the right hand of the person on your left. Try it and you'll see how it works!

SPELLING BEE

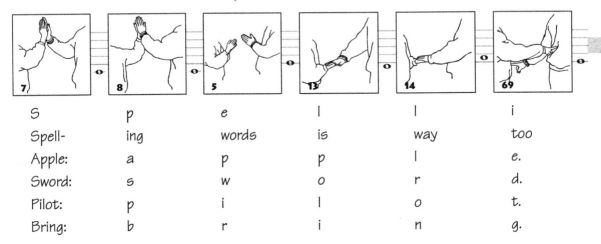

S	p	e	l	l	i
Spell-	ing	words	is	way	too
Apple:	a	p	p	l	e.
Sword:	s	w	o	r	d.
Pilot:	p	i	l	o	t.
Bring:	b	r	i	n	g.

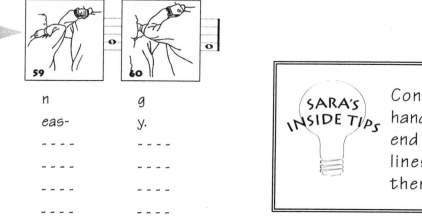

n

g

eas-

y.

- - - -

- - - -

- - - -

- - - -

- - - -

- - - -

- - - -

- - - -

SARA'S INSIDE TIPS Continue doing the hand motions at the end of the last four lines even though there aren't any

SPELLING BEE

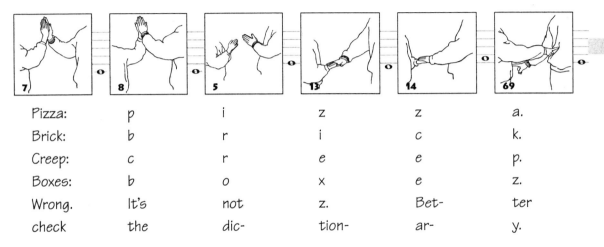

7	8	5	13	14	69
Pizza:	p	i	z	z	a.
Brick:	b	r	i	c	k.
Creep:	c	r	e	e	p.
Boxes:	b	o	x	e	z.
Wrong.	It's	not	z.	Bet-	ter
check	the	dic-	tion-	ar-	y.

SARA'S
INSIDE TIPS

Don't forget! Keep up the hand motions at the ends of the lines!

SPRING CLEANING

MORE VERSES

 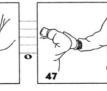 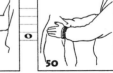

49	45	16	47	15	50
Time	to	do	spring	clean-	ing
Let's	start	with	the	clos-	et.
There's	a	junk	de-	pos-	it
Watch	out	for	what's	lean-	ing
A-	gainst	the	clos-	et	door.
O-	pen	it	up	and	crash
You're	in	a	heap	of	trash:
Smel-	ly	shoes,	ap-	ple	core,
Pink	ear-	ring,	wait	there's	more:

118

Spring Cleaning (continued)

Bowl-	ing	ball,	base-	ball	bat,
Ba-	by	dolls,	my	friend's	cat,
Cof-	fee	mug,	a	chess	rook,
Can-	dy	bar,	fish-	ing	hook,
Pic-	ture	frame,	pop	bot-	tle,
Hock-	ey	stick,	spy	nov-	el,
Com-	ic	strip,	vid-	e-	o
Chew-	ing	gum,	old	yo-	yo,
Let's	go	off	to	the	mall,
I'll	just	clean	up	next	fall.

Take Out the Trash

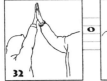

Take	out	the	trash	trash	trash.
Make	up	your	bed	bed	bed.
That's	what	they	said	said	said.
I	went	out-	side	side	side
To	ride	my	bike	bike	bike.
That's	what	I	like	like	like.
I	saw	a	cow	cow	cow.
He	blurt-	ed	moo	moo	moo.

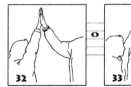   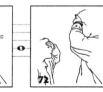

32	33	32	72	73	72
He	saw	me	too	too	too.
Next	to	the	store	store	store.
I	bought	a	pie	pie	pie.
I	said	good-	bye	bye	bye.
Next	to	the	park	park	park
To	climb	and	slide	slide	slide.
Play	seek	and	hide	hide	hide.

TEDDY BEAR

MORE VERSES

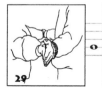 o o o o o 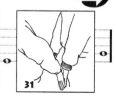 o

Ted-	dy	bear	just	ar-	rived.
Ted-	dy	bear	come	a-	live.
Ted-	dy	bear	turn	a-	round.
Ted-	dy	bear	touch	the	ground.
Ted-	dy	bear	blink	your	eye.

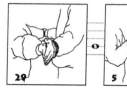   

Ted-	dy	bear	tell	me	"Hi!"
Ted-	dy	bear	run	up	stairs.
Ted-	dy	bear	say	your	prayers.
Ted-	dy	bear	turn	the	light.
Ted-	dy	bear	say	good-	night.

TOGETHER

    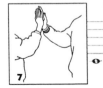

7	70	28	8	71	30
Sun	comes	up,	moon	goes	down,
Busy	in	city,	calm	in	town,
Black	is	dark,	white	is	light,
Peace	is	calm,	war	is	fight,
Ground	and	foot,	sky	and	head,
Pen	and	ink,	pen-	cil	lead,
T.	V.	view,	words	in	book,
Big	o-	cean,	skin-	ny	brook,

124

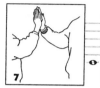   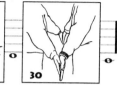

Fax	mach-	ine,	tel-	e-	phone,
Pop-	sic-	cle,	ice	cream	cone,
Sneeze	pep-	per,	thirst-	y	salt,
Root	beer	float,	choco-	late	malt,
One	pen-	ny,	five	and	dime,
Sour	lem-	on,	tang-	y	lime,
To-	geth-	er	for-	ev-	er.

TWELVE MONTHS

 o o o o o  o

Thir-	ty	days	has	Sep-	tem-
Ap-	ril,	June,	and	No-	vem-
All	the	rest	have	thir-	ty
Ex-	cept	Feb-	ru-	ar-	y,
And	that	has	twen-	ty	eight
And	twen-	ty	nine	in	leap

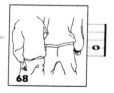

ber,
ber.
one.
Fun!
clear
year.

SARA'S INSIDE TIPS

You'll never confuse the number of days in a month after you learn this game!

TWO BUCKS

MORE VERSES

When	the	day	is	yucks,
Mom	gives	us	two	bucks.
We	get	to	spend	it
how-	ev-	er	we	want.
Ice	cream	cones?		
Chick-	en	bones?		
Piz-	za	slice?		
Cou-	ple	dice?		
Star	pos-	ter?		

128

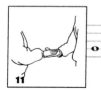   

Roller	coas-	ter?	
Toy	whis-	tle?	
Water	pis-	tol?	
We	looked	a-	round
But	none	we	found.
It	got	too	late
to	hes-	i-	tate.
So	two	bucks	(Thanks!)
for	pig-	gy	banks!

UMPIRE STATE BUILDING

MORE VERSES

9	10	20	68	22	23
My	friend	said,	"Come	o-	ver."
I	asked	my	mom	and	dad,
And	they	told	me,	"Yes,	you
Can	full	of	red	so-	da
Pop-	corn	in	the	mov-	ies,
Big	wide	pic-	ture	on	the
Screen	door	keeps	all	the	bugs
"Out	on	strikes"	yelled	the	Ump-

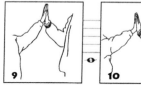					
9	10	20	68	22	23
Pire	state	build-	ing	tall	and
"Hi"	you	say	to	greet	some-
One	is	less	than	sev-	en,
Sev-	en's	less	than	thir-	ty
To	the	mall	we	went,	but
our	mo-	ney	was	spent	all-
"Ready	for	the	game?"	said	coach
"We	got-	ta	win	to-	day."

UNCLE MOYER

MORE VERSES

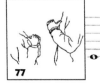

My	un-	cle	Moyer
Owns	a	toy	store.
He	gives	me	all
sorts	of	good	stuff:
A	fire	en-	gine
With	a	red	light
Long	reels	of	string
And	drag-	on	kite
A	ba-	by	doll

Uncle Moyer (continued)

 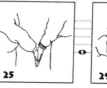

A	bas-	ket-	ball
A	tram-	po-	line
Some	jell-	y	beans.
Oh	well,	I	sup-
pose	I	should	tell
My	un-	cle	Moyer's
Just	a	law-	yer.

WHAT'S YOUR NAME?

MORE VERSES

 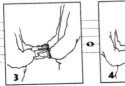 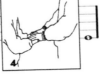

What's	your	name?
John-	ny	Toad.
Where's	your	house?
Down	the	road.
What	ad-	dress?
Wa-	ter	cress.
What's	your	age?
That's	to	guess.

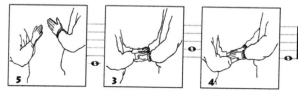

What's	your	name?
Sun-	ny	Rain.
Where's	your	house?
The	next	lane.
What	add-	ress?
Ends	with	fours.
What's	your	age?
Same	as	yours.

When I Grow Up

  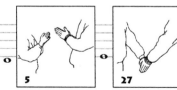

34   36   5   27

Bank-	ers	lend,	
Law-	yers	de-	fend,
Doc-	tors	re-	pair,
Nurs-	es	care,	
Pi-	lots	fly,	
Dish-	wash-	ers	dry,
Man-	a-	gers	boss,

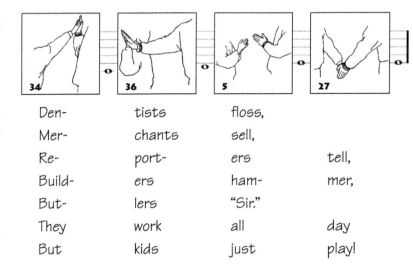

Den-	tists	floss,	
Mer-	chants	sell,	
Re-	port-	ers	tell,
Build-	ers	ham-	mer,
But-	lers	"Sir."	
They	work	all	day
But	kids	just	play!

WORLD TOUR

     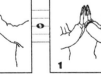

28	29	30	32	33	1
Miss	Beck-	y's	sup-	er	to-
She	fixed	the	Lean-	ing	Tow-
Climb-	ed	the	Eif-	fel	Tow-
Washed	win-	dows	of	Sears	Tow-
She	stared	at	the	Par-	then-
Rode	the	sub-	way	in	Jap-
Froze	in	Red	Square	in	Mos-

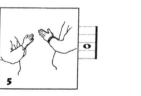

ur:

er,

er,

er.

on,

an,

cow.

SARA'S INSIDE TIPS

On the words "Leaning Tower," lean in toward your friend!

28	29	30	32	33	1
She	ran	from	mad	bulls	in
Chased	Af-	ri-	can	el-	e-
Ate	fat	waf-	fles	in	Bel-
She	set	her	watch	to	Big
Made	sand-	cast-	les	in	huge
Drove	on	Ger-	man	aut-	o-
Beck-	y's	trip	was	just	one
It	end-	ed	when	she	woke

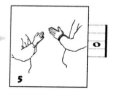

Spain,
phants,
gium.
Ben,
dunes,
bahn.
night.
up.

SARA'S INSIDE TIPS

Teach your parents how to hand-clap! You can have fun together!

CREATE YOUR OWN

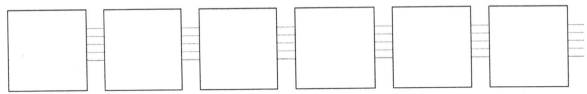

If you know or create some great hand-clapping games, send them to me!
I may use them in future editions of this book. My address is:

Sara Bernstein
c/o Adams Media Corporation
260 Center Street
Holbrook, MA 02343

(All submissions become the property of the author.)

ABOUT THE AUTHOR

Sara Bernstein speeds through her neighborhood on Rollerblades, torments her brother by composing rock songs on the piano, and drags her family to Disneyland whenever she gets a chance. Now twelve years old, Sara lives in sunny Scottsdale, Arizona.